Jessica,

God will do it!

Blessings!

[signature]

1/1/20

BREAKING FORTH

A Release into Your Kairos Season

Dr. Angela M. Rucker

authorHOUSE

AuthorHouse™
1663 Liberty Drive
Bloomington, IN 47403
www.authorhouse.com
Phone: 1 (800) 839-8640

© 2019 Dr. Angela M. Rucker. All rights reserved.

No part of this book may be reproduced, stored in a retrieval system, or transmitted by any means without the written permission of the author.

Published by AuthorHouse 08/20/2019

ISBN: 978-1-7283-2378-7 (sc)
ISBN: 978-1-7283-2377-0 (e)

Library of Congress Control Number: 2019912174

Print information available on the last page.

Any people depicted in stock imagery provided by Getty Images are models, and such images are being used for illustrative purposes only.
Certain stock imagery © Getty Images.

Scripture taken from The Holy Bible, King James Version. Public Domain

This book is printed on acid-free paper.

Because of the dynamic nature of the Internet, any web addresses or links contained in this book may have changed since publication and may no longer be valid. The views expressed in this work are solely those of the author and do not necessarily reflect the views of the publisher, and the publisher hereby disclaims any responsibility for them.

Contents

Foreword xi
Preface xiii
Acknowledgments xvii
Introduction xix

Chapter 1   Sanctioned for Dominion 1
Chapter 2   The Power of Self-Discovery 9
Chapter 3   Unlocking Your Potential 16
Chapter 4   It's the Right Time 26
Chapter 5   Hidden Greatness 34
Chapter 6   In the Rough 43
Chapter 7   Victory Shine 50
Chapter 8   The Rewards of Diligence 58

Epilogue 69
About the Author 75

To all those who struggle to break forth
from self-imposed shackles.

Enlarge the place of thy tent, and let them stretch forth the curtains of thine habitations: spare not, lengthen thy cords, and strengthen thy stakes;

For thou shalt break forth on the right hand and on the left...

—Isaiah 54:2-3 (KJV)

Kairos Season

A season of change when the supernatural hand of God orchestrates that time should intersect with divine opportunities to accommodate divine purpose.

It's a defining season that catapults you into your prophetic destiny.

FOREWORD

Breaking Forth is written with the honesty and transparency required for true deliverance and freedom. It underscores how easy it is to become entangled by ourselves, which means we need untangling by the power of God. This book will set everyone free, anyone free.

Dr. Angela Rucker really captures the experience of a person who has become trapped in a terrible circumstance and struggles to understand what the exit for life might be. All of us can easily lose touch with who we are when we feel as though people define us by what we have done.

Breaking Forth really touches on how our raw human experience can restrict us from being who God really created us to be. Without someone showing us the way, opening the door to freedom, or teaching us how to break free from our entrapments, hope plays no role, and faith is hindered.

Dr. Angela Rucker pours out her deepest and wisest thinking, which will bless many and deliver thousands from unidentified strongholds and traps. It speaks openly and candidly about the demonic tools that the enemy uses to cause us to be distracted from what God has placed in us.

When you read *Breaking Forth*, it will release what has been held up for you by showing you that the power within you is greater than anything confronting you.

Bishop PJ Edmund Sr.

PREFACE

I give all praise and honor to my Lord and Savior, Jesus Christ. I give thanks to the Holy Spirit for His enabling power.

Breaking forth is a testimony of my own struggle to emancipate myself from the self-imposed shackles that I allowed to imprison me for many years. I was blind to the transforming power of God that was available to me. I thank God for opening my eyes when he did. For years, I stumbled around in the prison of darkness. I was like the ship on the ocean without a compass. When I reflect and I remember some of the choices I made in my own life, which I live to tell about, I know that God is a loving God.

My priority had nothing to do with God. Life in the fast lane was the thrust of my life. You name it, I did it. What was seemingly fun was always challenged by my desire to discover self. I was having fun, but there was an emptiness that lived inside me, and little did I know that the emptiness could only be filled if I allowed God to be in control of my life. I thought I had all the answers. I totally depended upon self-government, and God was not on my radar.

I knew about God. I knew that he was the creator of heaven and earth and he was the giver of all life. I knew about the virgin birth and that Jesus was the Savior of the world. I was familiar with prayer, and on many occasions, I engaged God in a conversation about my needs. I read the Bible and was particularly comforted with the Psalms. From time to time, I would go to church, and I would leave just as empty as I entered.

However, as much as I thought I knew about God, and as much as I would periodically engage Him in long talks about me, I never knew Him. I did not have an intimate relationship with Him.

It was July 29, 1989, when I came to a place in my life where I realized that I needed God. That was the night I accepted Jesus Christ as my personal Savior and made a commitment to serve Him for the rest of my life. Something inexplicable happened when I gave my life to Christ. It was as though God had literally taken His fingers and opened my eyes.

At the time I gave my life to Christ, I felt a compulsion to break free from self-imposed ignorance to discover the me I could become. I was desperate to *break forth* from ignorance and shame. I hungered and thirsted for the freedom to live a life that was consistent with the purpose for which I was born. I just knew that I needed God.

There was such a great emptiness on the inside of me and nothing that I tried was able to fill the void. I knew that there was more to my life than what I had lived. Now that I had surrendered my life to Christ, the eyes of my understanding were opened. I could now read the Bible and walk away with understanding of the word of God. God began to reveal His mysteries to me.

One Saturday morning, in March 1990, I had an encounter with God that is forever etched in my memory. I was driving on the highway, and God gave me a special visitation. It was as though God hijacked my car, and I ended up in a remote parking lot miles away from my house. The Shekinah glory of God fell in the car. I was caught up in a zone that was foreign to me. In a vision, I saw a globe that came out of heaven. There was a ribbon wrapped around the globe, and on the ribbon was written, "My brother's keeper." The globe jetted across the sky, and finally it landed on a building, and the ribbon left the globe and was stretched out above the door of the building.

I will never forget the echoing voice that spoke with so much authority as God commanded me to preach His gospel—"Go preach my gospel." My response was just like Jeremiah's. God and I pretty much had the same conversation, and I was no match for God. I cried so hard as I fearfully surrendered and answered "yes" to the call of God.

I was weakened by the power of God, and after about one hour of just bawling, I humbly made my way home at about 10 miles per hour. When I got home, I got on my knees in front of my bed, and the Spirit of God put me to sleep. I slept for about four hours on my knees.

When I awoke, it was as though I were in a new land. Everything looked fresh and new. To my surprise, while I was asleep, God had downloaded sermons in me, and new words were introduced to my vocabulary.

From that day, I gave myself to God, and I have allowed God to raise me up according to His plan for my life. I trusted God with my life and still do. Now, as I look back over my Christian walk, I am amazed at how God has directed the course of my life.

I am married to a wonderful man of God, Apostle

Benjamin W. Rucker. I serve as the assistant pastor of Bride of Christ Church Ministries, Int'l. We oversee churches all over the world. So many lives have been changed as God uses us to minister globally.

Each day, I renew my commitment to be used by God for His purpose. God has directed my path across several continents to minister healing and restoration to the lost. He has taken me beyond geographical boundaries to preach and teach the gospel of Jesus Christ. Many have come to know the saving knowledge of the Lord, Jesus Christ.

Cradle of H.O.P.E. is a foundation that God directed me to start. Needy children all over the world benefit from this foundation.

I have given my life away to Jesus, and I trust Him to continue to lead me as I press forward into the *kairos season* to complete my prenatal assignment—a prophet to the nations.

Break forth!

Acknowledgments

All praise and honor to the Lord God Almighty, who gives me the strength to keep on going,

To my church family, Bride of Christ Church Ministries. Thank you for your love and support.

To the children of Cradle of H.O.P.E., Inc., all over the world, who inspire me to reach out and touch.

To Dr. Geneva Henderson, who has stuck by me through thick and thin. Thank you for your patience and unwavering dedication to the Gospel of Christ.

Last but not least, to my wonderful husband, Bennie, who continues to encourage me with loving kindness and leads by example. Thank you for being a living example of Christ. Every day, you give me more reasons to love you.

Introduction

There are times in your life when you must disembark or make an exit so you can enter a prescribed place that leads to your destiny. Personally, I am never excited about having to leave my area of comfort to go somewhere new. I struggle with letting go and embracing the unfamiliar. I wrestle with God all the time about sudden departures. However, I have come to realize that I have manifold blessings that can be activated when I leave where I am and go to where I need to be. I must purposefully let go of my own personal agenda and surrender to the will of God.

Historically, God has proven Himself to be the greatest trip organizer there could ever be. He orchestrates and demonstrates with great accuracy. He supernaturally commands the agenda of heaven to coincide and connect with the necessities of earth. He commands and directs the times—*kairos* and *chronos*. He is intentional about His directives and has established a pattern of bringing you out to bring you in. Not only does He summon you to leave but He provides for the trip you are about to take. He gives you the vision and He sends the provisions for the journey.

Breaking Forth speaks to a series of departures and arrivals. It is about moving from places of obscurity to places of prominence. It is no longer about being comfortable in a place you want to be but being positionally correct—where God wants you to be. No longer will you have to accept negativity as your portion. You are moving into a season of increase and saying goodbye to the reign of mediocrity.

Your change has come and you are now being released into a season of divine orchestrations. You are being summoned to spread your wings and soar into heights you have never ascended to before.

As you read the pages of this book, be prepared to meet the person you have never met before—the real you. Be ready to experience a shift in your mental assessment of self.

Breaking forth demands that you disconnect and separate yourself from entanglements and weights that will try to prevent you from moving forward. What you think was dead will suddenly begin to kick. There is a revival that has been supernaturally directed to anchor in your soul. Mental shackles shall fall off, and you shall no longer be restricted and imprisoned by the thoughts of your own mind.

There is a revival that has been supernaturally directed to anchor in your soul.

The control tower has cleared you for take-off and it has been forecasted in heaven that there shall be no atmospheric turbulence. Your flight pattern has been set and God has already cleared your path. You have been approved and released to *break forth* into your *kairos season* of transformation. You have been granted access to the vault of hidden treasures of divine wealth and richness. Heaven is on standby to release whatever you need for this leg of your journey.

The *breaking forth* is orchestrated by the release of divine power which is designed to deliver those in captivity and break the bonds of mental slavery. The supernatural power of Almighty God shall prevail against anything that comes to sabotage your destiny.

You shall enter a season of expansion and you shall *break forth* on the right and on the left.

Your testimony shall be great!

It shall be well!

Chapter 1

SANCTIONED FOR DOMINION

As you navigate your way through the pages of this book, I celebrate with you as you *break forth* into your destiny. May the revelation of who you were born to be arrest your spirit and your consciousness. May you say goodbye to a life of mediocrity that was never meant to be yours and *break forth* into the destiny that was ordained for you.

For something to *break forth*, there must be a release of power in a direction. It is a breaking away from a place of captivity or restraint. Almighty God has made provision for every believer to break forth into purpose. He has given us authority and has sanctioned us to live with significance and be all that we can be.

Breaking forth is becoming all that you can be through the process of ascending to levels beyond your present station. It is being able to operate with dominion.

Breaking forth is becoming all that you can be through the process of ascending to levels beyond your present station.

The Bible is the inspired and the inerrant word of God, which gives us timeless teachings upon which to build our lives. It is our divine constitution for living here on earth. It defines who we are, tells us our rights, and reveals our covenants. Most importantly, the Bible is God's revelation of Himself.

The Bible gives us the dominion mandate that outlines God's expectation of us as we occupy our different realms of authority. First, it defines you, and then it tells you what you can do according to God's manifest power, which resides in you. It clearly reveals that every person has been sanctioned by God to have dominion.

In the book of Genesis, we are given the first commandment that God gave to humankind.

> *And God said, Let us make man in our image, after our likeness: and let them have dominion over the fish of the sea, and over the fowl of the air, and over the cattle, and over all the earth, and over every creeping thing that creepeth upon the earth. So God created man in his own image, in the image of God created he him; male and female created he them. And God blessed them, and God said unto them, Be fruitful, and multiply, and replenish the earth, and subdue it: and have dominion over the fish of the sea, and over the fowl of the air, and over every living thing that moveth upon the earth.* **(Genesis 1:26–28 KJV)**

When God spoke the universe into existence, it was the creative power of God's word that formed the world. It was with that same creative power that God declared our identity into being and sanctioned dominion as the destiny of men and women in the earth realm.

The interesting thing about it is that while God made a declaration that was corporately intended, He designed each person uniquely. There are more than 7 billion people on the planet, and yet no one other than you has your fingerprint. God declared your identity unique in the beginning when He established the dominion mandate. God didn't wait to put this in the middle of the Bible or the end of the Bible. He strategically placed it in the beginning so you and I could know that God's initial plan for us was tied to His dominion mandate.

The word "dominion" in Hebrew is *radah*. It is a word that speaks to royalty. Here are some further definitions of *radah*:

- Rule
- Reign
- Sovereignty
- Prevail against

> *But ye are a chosen generation, a royal priesthood, a holy nation, a peculiar people; that ye should shew forth the praises of him who hath called you out of darkness into his marvelous light.* **(1 Peter 2:9 KJV)**

God gave males and females the right and responsibility to rule in their roles and to govern with authority. God's plan is that every human being exercises the dominion mandate. You should dominate anything that is trying to oppress and subjugate you.

You have been given the authority to *break forth* from shackles that are holding you down and causing you to live beneath biblical constitutional principles. God has released timeless principles in His word that are designed to elevate you to your highest level of life. You are authorized to tread upon and prevail against any forces that seek to keep you captive.

> *Behold, I give unto you power to tread on serpents and scorpions, and over all the power of the enemy: and nothing shall by any means hurt you.* **(Luke 10:19)**

You can prevail against any subversive element that comes to destroy you. Inherent in the dominion mandate is the assurance that no weapon formed against you shall prosper.

To have dominion means that you operate according to the governmental rule and the code of conduct of God's kingdom. There is a kingdom culture that you must embrace to break forth as a kingdom ambassador.

God has given us keys to access this realm of divine authority and occupy as kingdom citizens. It means that you operate according to kingdom protocol to bear kingdom representation. The word of God outlines all protocols that will allow you to break forth into dominion.

Dominion is an action word. The first two letters of the word spell *do.* This means that you must execute, implement, perform, and fulfill specific requirements that would reflect good success in your life. To live a victorious life, your action plan should be consistent with the dominion mandate.

To live a victorious life, your action plan should be consistent with the dominion mandate.

> *But be ye doers of the word, and not hearers only, deceiving your own selves. For if any be a hearer of the word, and not a doer, he is like unto a man beholding his natural face in a glass: For he beholdeth himself, and goeth his way, and straightway forgetteth what manner of man he was. But whoso looketh into the perfect law of liberty, and continueth therein, he being not a forgetful hearer, but a doer of the work, this man shall be blessed in his deed.*
> **(James 1:22–25 KJV)**

When you operate in dominion, you become a practitioner of the word of God. Every choice that you make will be aligned with kingdom principles set forth in the dominion mandate.

The word of God tells us that we are made in the image and after the likeness of God. That means that we should live in a manner that is consistent with the character of God. Absence of dominion will always present evidence of a damaged character. A flawed character has violated the code of conduct that is in accordance with the dominion mandate. When you violate the dominion mandate, you cannot *be fruitful, multiply, fill the earth, and subdue it.*

A flawed character has violated the code of conduct that is in accordance with the dominion mandate.

Breaking forth implies that there is a change of mind-set that unshackles you from mediocrity and the acceptance of a substandard life. You must *break forth* from the misguided myths that label you incapable of extraordinary achievements and accomplishments. You must *break forth* from every yoke of bondage and wear your royal robe of liberty and truth.

You must break forth from the misguided myths that label you incapable of extraordinary achievements and accomplishments.

God has sanctioned your dominion. It was never God's plan for you to accept defeat. You have the delegated authority to be fruitful, to multiply, to replenish, and to subdue. God gave you the authority to rise above every circumstance that comes to rob you of your liberty.

God's plan was never for you to be an insignificant specimen. You are the royalty of God. A substandard life was never the portion that God set aside for you. You are His handiwork and His great treasure. God wants you to live a royal life that commands great influence on earth.

> *But ye are a chosen generation, a royal priesthood, an holy nation, a peculiar people; that ye should shew forth the praises of him who hath called you out of darkness into his marvelous light: Which in time past were not a people but are now the people of God: which had not obtained mercy, but now have obtained mercy.* **(1 Peter 2:9–10 KJV)**

After Satan tricked Eve into disobeying God in the garden of Eden, Adam and Eve were evicted and dethroned. They were discharged from their roles as caretakers of God's business. The fellowship between humans and God was broken. Satan thought he had won the battle, but God had another plan that would reconcile people back to God.

> *And the LORD God said unto the serpent, Because thou hast done this, thou art cursed above all cattle, and above every beast of the field; upon thy belly shalt thou go, and dust shalt thou eat all the days of thy life: And I will put enmity between thee and the woman, and between thy seed and her seed; it shall bruise thy head, and thou shalt bruise his heel.* **(Genesis 3:14–15 KJV)**

God is a promise keeper. He kept His word, and the devil was defeated on Calvary's cross through the crucifixion and resurrection of Jesus Christ. The shed blood of Jesus Christ paid the price for our redemption. Now, because of Jesus, you can *break forth* in dominion. You can live a life of victory. You don't have to walk around in shackles and in chains.

You can be the conqueror God created you to be. Take dominion over your circumstances, and never let them dominate you. You were born for greatness. The original mold that God created was the perfect workmanship of God. You were born to live the dominion life of victory. You can *break forth* into your *kairos season* of extraordinary accomplishments, which will take you to higher heights and deeper depths.

> *Enlarge the place of thy tent, and let them stretch forth the curtains of thine habitations: spare not, lengthen thy cords, and strengthen thy stakes; For thou shalt break forth on the right hand and on the left.* **(Isaiah 54:2–3 KJV)**

You have been sanctioned by Almighty God to do great exploits on earth. Greatness is your portion and your time to soar is now. You can go beyond where you are and ascend into heights that will bring you into a greater revelation of who God is and who you are in His plan for humanity. You are God's masterpiece who has been tagged to be a great representation of God in the realm of the earth.

Breaking forth is the will of God for you!

Chapter 2

THE POWER OF SELF-DISCOVERY

One of the most self-defeating states to be in is the state of ignorance about who you really are. So many people are led to believe that wanting more than they presently have is a weakness and not a strength. So, as a result, they accept where they are in life as their final destination. Discovering who you are from God's perspective is the first step in discovering who you can become. If you do not know who you are, you will allow others to define you. Acceptance of a life that is punctuated by defeat and lack is not God's plan for citizens of His kingdom.

Beloved, I wish above all things that thou mayest prosper and be in health, even as thy soul prospereth. **(3 John 1:2 KJV)**

It is impossible to live an authentic life without discovering the real you. You can be the world's best discoverer and discover all the ways to go back and forth to the moon by launching great spaceships but your greatest discovery is when you discover self. You are forced to be someone else if you have not yet discovered self. The real you will never get a chance to surface without self-discovery.

Your greatest discovery is when you discover self.

Self-discovery is the process by which you become acquainted with the "you" that is living in obscurity. The imprisoned dreams that were never allowed to materialize into a grand reality of achievements have been waiting to break forth. The earth is crying out for a release of greatness from those who are destined to have dominion over the earth. There is a treasure of greatness embedded on the inside of you and you are obligated to release it into the earth realm.

There are gifts embedded inside you. Your gifts make way for you to be sought after by many. Self-discovery allows you to recognize your gift. Unless you discover self, you will meander through life without ever meeting the real you.

One of the most important truths about you is that you are not an afterthought in the mind of God. Deep down, on the inside, you are insulated with goodness and greatness. You are a masterpiece of God's love. The best of God is in you, and He made you without using inferior parts.

The best of God is in you and it can only be released when you discover self.

I will praise thee; for I am fearfully and wonderfully made: marvelous are thy works; and that my soul knoweth right well. **(Psalm 139:14 KJV)**

Because of the ignorance of our real identity, we have acquired and accepted a disfigured and blemished image of who we are. So many people suffer from depression, delusion, and confusion because they don't know who they are from God's perspective.

The very breath of God insulates you on the inside. Your value is priceless and you have the capacity to *break forth* into greatness. You are a triune masterpiece—mind, body, and spirit. You are the excellence of God's workmanship. You are exquisitely designed by the best designer and wondrously built with amazing capabilities.

You are exquisitely designed by the best designer and wondrously built with amazing capabilities.

After all that God had made, it wasn't until he made man (male and female) that He was satisfied with His creation project. Everything was good in the eyes of God, but after God made male and female, He approved His workmanship in the superlative—He said it was very good. You are the excellence of God.

And God saw everything that he had made, and, behold, it was very good. **(Genesis 1:31 KJV)**

Self-discovery allows you to connect with God's purpose for your life so you can *break forth* in dominion and live your best life. When you walk in dominion, you can take hold of your covenant rights and benefits. You can live the abundant life now and not postpone living until you get to heaven. The devil's plan is to get you so confused about who really are so you will live a life of defeat. His plan is to infuse your mind with thoughts that devalue your worth and cause you to live a life that lacks direction and purpose.

The world is full of so many who have bought into the deceptive lies of the devil and are walking in defeat because they are ignorant of their indigenous character and they do not know who they are from God's perspective. The Bible clearly states that believers are positioned in Christ Jesus. It declares that, in Christ, you are above and not beneath. The book of Genesis reveals that you are made in the image and likeness of God. The Bible further declares that you are certifiably adopted in the body of Christ.

> *For as many as are led by the Spirit of God, they are the sons of God. For ye have not received the spirit of bondage again to fear; but ye have received the Spirit of adoption, whereby we cry, Abba, Father.* **(Romans 8:14–15 KJV)**

So many who are born again profess Jesus to be their Lord and Savior, and yet, they govern their lives in such a way that reflects ignorance of their true identity. Your real identity is not determined by a socioeconomic status. It's not determined by academic credentials; nor is it measured by societal norms. Economics, academics, and societal norms were not the underlying criteria that God used in creating you.

The essence of who you are is not determined by any natural phenomenon. You came out of God.

Economics, academics, and societal norms were not the underlying criteria that God used in creating you.

God, in His infinite wisdom, knows the purpose for everything that He creates, and He purposefully equips whatever He creates with the necessary character that supports the purpose of his creation.

- Birds have wings so that they can fly.
- Fish have gills because they live in water.

These animals function according to their identity, and their character supports their purpose.

God is an amazing God and He is intentional about His creation. You were in God before you were born. God released you into the earth realm with an identity that uniquely represents Him. Even when God created the earth, He was intentional in His works:

- The sun shines in the day.
- The moon and the stars illuminate the night.
- The grass blankets the earth.
- The rain waters the vegetation.
- The ocean produces more than half the oxygen in the atmosphere.

God makes no mistake with the character, dimensions, or the intent of anything He creates.

God intentionally made you and You are not a mistake.

One of the most disturbing realities about the Body of Christ is that many Christians do not know who they are, and as a result, they operate out of character. There is an identity crisis that is pervasive throughout Christendom, which has produced a community of dysfunctional people.

Personality disorders have affected people who profess to be sons and daughters of Christ.

If you know who you are from God's perspective, you can live and conduct your affairs according to God's distinct purpose for your life and in a manner that is an excellent representation of God. When you know who you are from God's perspective, you do not seek validation from man.

When you know who you are from God's perspective, you do not seek validation from man.

Many Christians get up every morning and their only hope for the day is that someone will validate them. They are ignorant of the noble truth that they have already been validated by God. They seek daily evaluation, daily recognition, and daily validation from man:

- The boss
- Friends
- Husbands
- Wives
- Significant others

As a result, they cannot function to the full level of their potential because they wait for approval from another human being. They become enslaved to the approval and validation of human beings. They are held captive and in shackles to the undervalued estimation of self that has been given to them by others.

> **The prison doors have been opened but they are bound and tied to the deflated imaginations of their own minds.**

They are enslaved because their minds are governed by the will of man and not the will of God. Ignorance of your real identity will cause you to act outside of the will of God. Many people are living in a parallel universe that is governed by laws contrary to the word of God.

> *And be not conformed to this world: but be ye transformed by the renewing of your mind, that ye may prove what is that good, and acceptable, and perfect, will of God.*
> **(Romans 12:2 KJV)**

Christians are majoring in lying, cheating, fornicating, drugging, sipping, smoking, and covering it up with "hallelujahs" and "praise the Lords" while they function below their full potential. Identity theft has left them to accept mediocrity and failure as their destiny.

My prayer is that Almighty God will dismantle every plan of the enemy that comes to hold you hostage and keep you in darkness about who you are. I bind up every word curse spoken over your life that is designed to distort the image of who you are.

I decree and declare that you will denounce every subliminal thought that would reduce or underestimate your value. The shackles of ignorance will not prevail in your life, and the knowledge of who you are from God's perspective will cause you to *break forth* into your destiny.

Chapter 3

UNLOCKING YOUR POTENTIAL

One of the greatest detriments to our growth and development in the kingdom of God is untapped potential that has been inactive and dormant in our lives. So many people have lived unfruitful and unfulfilled lives because they have not unlocked the door to the great reservoir of ability that lies within.

Submerged in every person are latent qualities or abilities that are unharnessed and untapped. Many have been denied the process of self-development and empowerment because they have not used the proper keys to unlock their potential. For you to *break forth* into your *kairos season,* there must be an unlocking of your potential that would expose your capacity to develop into a better version of yourself. The prophetic destiny of every person can only be realized when you optimize the measure of your potential. Good success is harvested when you can untether your potential so ideas and concepts can be converted into tangible evidence of your efforts.

> ***For you to break forth into your kairos season, there must be an unlocking of your potential that would expose your capacity to develop into a better version of yourself.***

So many people are living their lives in a box of self-imposed darkness. There is so much locked away on the inside of every man and woman who seeks to move from obscurity into a permanent position of prominence. However, of the more than 7 billion people on planet Earth, very few have maximized what God has graciously blessed them with.

In the biblical constitution that was laid out for man in the beginning, evidence of fruitfulness was a prerequisite. It is impossible to be fruitful without unlocking your potential.

> *And God blessed them, and God said unto them, Be fruitful, and multiply, and replenish the earth, and subdue it: and have dominion over the fish of the sea, and over the fowl of the air, and over every living thing that moveth upon the earth.* **(Genesis 1:28 KJV)**

It was never God's plan for us to be impotent and unproductive. The journey into our *kairos season* requires unleashing of our abilities to accommodate the prophetic blueprint for our lives. How you live your life is a statement of how much of your potential you have unlocked. A life that is punctuated by victory and success is one that has opened the door to its full potential.

> ***How you live your life is a statement of how much of your potential you have unlocked.***

It is not what you have done; it is about what you are yet able to do. It is about where you are going and the rest of your journey. It is *breaking forth* from a self-imposed prison of under achievement to a new dimension of self-development. There are no limits to how far you can extend your mind. The extent of your potential is not measured by or limited to the opinion of another human being. Only Almighty God Himself knows the latitude and the longitude of your potential and the extent of your capacity—He knows the depth and breadth. He has deposited things in you that you are yet to release. The full measure of your potential is found in the bosom of God's divine providence. What He has put in you is boundless and unlimited. He has already given you the capacity to stretch beyond the status quo and all self-imposed limitations.

> *But as it is written, Eye hath not seen, nor ear heard, neither have entered into the heart of man, the things which God hath prepared for them that love him.*
> **(1 Corinthians 2:9 KJV)**

Whenever God is getting ready to elevate and expand you, the enemy will try to disrupt the plan of God for your life. There is a network of underground conspirators, imps and demons, who have been dispatched from hell to vigilantly block your progress. They use subversive means to derail and sabotage your destiny.

> *Be sober, be vigilant; because your adversary the devil, as a roaring lion, walketh about, seeking whom he may devour.*
> **(1 Peter 5:8 KJV)**

Your adversary, the devil, knows that if your potential is unleashed, you are unstoppable. So he uses the naysayers to tell you that you can't. He uses the unbelievers to tell you that your vision is impossible. He uses all manner of discouragement to keep you from unlocking your potential. His plan is to subjugate you and bring you under his domination or control. He wants to enslave you and crush your desire for greatness because hell knows who you are and the greatness that is within you.

One of the greatest truths that you need to internalize is that you came out of God. The potential you have cannot be considered apart from God.

> *And God said, Let us make man in our image, after our likeness: and let them have dominion over the fish of the sea, and over the fowl of the air, and over the cattle, and over all the earth, and over every creeping thing that creepeth upon the earth. So God created man in his own image, in the image of God created he him; male and female created he them.* **(Genesis 1:26–27 KJV)**

You were created in the very image and likeness of God. You are the crown and summit of God's creation. You are the one to whom God has given His Spirit—His very own immortal breath.

You did not get here by accident. God purposefully dispatched you to the earthly realm to occupy until He comes. The wonderful thing is that when God released you into the earthly realm, He did not send you here empty. You arrived with a great reservoir of potential. God had already tagged you for a great assignment here on earth, and He measured out the potential that you would need.

> **You did not get here by accident. God purposefully dispatched you to the earthly realm to occupy until he comes.**

So many people are locked in the boundaries of a mundane world and never enter into the *kairos season* of divine engagement because of locked-up potential. Their lives are so humdrum, ordinary, and void of fulfillment.

For you to function according to the measure of your potential, you must attach yourself to your source. It is imperative that you detach yourself from people and attach yourself to God. Man is not your source—God is. Attachment to your source is the fuel that is needed for you to *break forth* into your *kairos season*. The Omnipotent God, creator of the universe, blew His breath into man, and man became a living soul. With His breath, the extent of man's potential was established.

> **It is imperative that you detach yourself from people and attach yourself to God.**

> And the LORD God formed man of the dust of the ground and breathed into his nostrils the breath of life; and man became a living soul. **(Genesis 2:7 KJV)**

You came out of God. You contain the potential of the source from which you came. Man can never determine how far you can go, because he is incapable of measuring the depth, the width, and the breadth of potential that God has placed in you. If you remain connected to your source, you will be empowered to be all that God has designed and purposed you to be.

The choice is yours as to how effective you want to be in the kingdom of God. You must decide if you want to be the best you or mediocre. You must decide if you want to remain stuck or if you want to go beyond self-limitation. You must decide if you want to be an original or a copy. Living a life of purpose or settling for mediocrity is your choice.

> *I call heaven and earth to record this day against you, that I have set before you life and death, blessing and cursing: therefore choose life, that both thou and thy seed may live.* **(Deuteronomy 30:19 KJV)**

When you tap into God, He reveals the blueprint of your life. He gives you revelations of the plans He has for you. He is the great architect who supernaturally sketches the blueprint to communicate His plan and purpose for your life. He lays out the design and provides the necessary tools to unlock your potential so dreams and visions can be realized.

When you tap into God, He reveals the blueprint of your life.

The Bible encourages us to make our requests known to God.

Jabez was not afraid to reveal the desire of his heart to God. You must have the mindset of Jabez and cry out for enlargement. You must be ready to let the hand of God rest upon you and take you wherever that enlargement might take you.

Breaking Forth

> *And Jabez called on the God of Israel, saying, oh that thou wouldest bless me indeed, and enlarge my coast, and that thine hand might be with me, and that thou wouldest keep me from evil, that it may not grieve me! And God granted him that which he requested.* **(1 Chronicles 4:10 KJV)**

To experience greater, you must be willing to enter the realm of the unknown. The same old techniques and efforts won't unlock anything for you today. You must want more of God and more from God. Potential that is not tested will go with you to the cemetery.

To experience greater, you must be willing to enter the realm of the unknown.

To unlock your potential, you must exercise your faith and do something that you have never done before. Put those latent qualities or abilities to work so that you can enjoy good success. The unlocking will not take place by osmosis. Potential is unlocked by deciding and doing whatever is conducive to support the purpose for whatever the potential is needed for. In other words, you must think it and then do it. The decision must be followed through with action that produces tangible evidence of your thoughts and ideas.

> *But wilt thou know, O vain man, that faith without works is dead?*
> **(James 2:20–21 KJV)**

A time will come when you will leave this earth to go to your final destination. You must make the resolve now that when they lower your coffin to put you in the grave, your potential will not be lowered with you.

It is your responsibility to empty yourself of everything that God gave you to deposit on earth. You must decide if you want to die with it or you want to leave a legacy on earth. When you leave a legacy on earth, your purpose exists even after your body is put in the grave. For all the years that you would have lived on planet Earth, what will you be remembered for that has impacted the lives of people. So many people die and never tap into their full potential because of mismanagement of the mind. They are victims of a thinking deficiency that has led them down the path of uselessness.

> **When you leave a legacy on earth, your purpose exists even after your body is put in the grave.**

When you think of yourself less than what God has created you to be, you will always be less than what you can become. If the greatness on the inside has never been released to live, you have given it permission to die within. You must not let the genius within you be ignored and buried under a blockade of negative thoughts and be laid to rest in a graveyard.

> **If the greatness on the inside has never been released to live, you have given it permission to die within.**

Fear is one of the greatest enemies of your potential. It stifles the greatness that is on the inside and leaves you void of purpose. It secretly devours you and, if not arrested, can leave you ineffective and impotent. Fear comes to incapacitate you and its aim is to prevent you from functioning in a normal way.

So many people are held captive by fear and their potential is locked in a dungeon of unproductivity. Your hopes, your dreams, and your visions are undone because fear has your potential locked up.

It is time to evict fear from your minds, your hearts, and your lives and live the abundant life that God has promised you. Fear will take up residence in any mind that welcomes it. It has dominion over all those who acquiesce to its rulership. Your portion is not to live a life that is governed by fear. Fear is the acceptance of self-imposed life imprisonment. There is a secret to living the fear-free life. Deliverance from fear is available through God.

> *I sought the LORD, and he heard me, and delivered me from all my fears.*
> **(Psalm 34:4 KJV)**

Fear will take up residence in any mind that welcomes it.

The faith in your heart must be bigger than the fear in your mind. You must kill your fear with action. Faith without works is dead. Do the thing you fear most and you will annihilate fear. When you start to do the things you fear most, you tear down invisible barriers that separate you from your destiny. Fear will always be around trying to tell you what you can't do but you must take dominion over your fear and tell it where to go. Send it back to hell from whence it came.

Do the thing you fear most and you will annihilate fear.

I am speaking to somebody who has been paralyzed by fear and stuck in a nonproductive zone. I dare you to do the thing you fear most. If fear has taken dominion over your life, I dare you to assassinate fear by taking the appropriate action.

Unlocking Your Potential

Another illegal resident of the mind is doubt. It is a major hindrance to unlocking your potential. Doubt about who God says you are and about what He says you can do distorts correct thinking and cultivates mental inertia. You were made to function by faith. The Bible declares to us that faith is the mechanism by which we should live our lives, and without such, it is impossible to please God.

Without faith it is impossible to please God. **(Hebrews 11:6)**

Faith is the antithesis of doubt.

- Doubt defines you as grasshopper, but faith declares that you are more than a conqueror.

- Doubt says, "You can only go but so far," while faith says, "There are no limits."

- Doubt says, "You will never make it to the top," and faith says, "Watch me soar."

- Doubt says, "God isn't going to do it," but faith says, "It is already done."

Whenever faith wins, doubt loses.

Break forth into your *kairos season*!

Chapter 4

IT'S THE RIGHT TIME

God orchestrates the time and seasons, and He orchestrates the timetable to facilitate His kingdom agenda. God lives outside of time. It is a bubble outside of eternity. God has favored you with this precious commodity to facilitate His purpose for your life.

Time cannot be bought or sold. It is given to us to use it, and if we do not use it, we lose it.

You might be among those who have been waiting for your season to change and have been wondering where God is. You have experienced some things in the past, and you are looking to God to change your situation. Be assured that God has not overlooked you. He has not neglected you; nor has He forgotten you. The divine favor of God is released according to God's plan and purpose for your life. God's timeline is based on His divine providence and His supreme sovereignty.

> *Daniel answered and said, Blessed be the name of God for ever and ever: for wisdom and might are his: And he changeth the times and the seasons:* **(Daniel 2:20–21 KJV)**

It's the Right Time

As you are reading this book, be encouraged: God has a plan for your life, and He has already measured out the degree and amount of favor that you need to accomplish His plan for your life. He knows where you are, and He knows where He is taking you. He has already mapped out your journey. He has already established your end from the beginning.

Your set time is synchronized to accommodate God's divine plan for your life and to introduce you to your *kairos season*. It's usually measured by *kairos* time and not *chronos* time, which refers to a chronological or sequential time. *Kairos* time refers to the opportune time. *Kairos* time is when the supernatural intersects with the natural.

The Bible says that there is a time for every season. It's interesting to note that even though God is outside of time, He controls time and will even interrupt time to set the time to release His divine favor upon your life. God holds a whole portfolio of your life with designated times to release divine favor upon you.

Man can do you a favor but only God can release favor upon your life. God is the great orchestrator of divine favor. God interrupts time to release His divine favor in His time. According to the Bible, it is not by might, and it is not by power but by His Spirit.

> *Then he answered and spake unto me, saying, This is the word of the LORD unto Zerubbabel, saying, Not by might, nor by power, but by my spirit, saith the LORD of hosts.* **(Zechariah 4:6 KJV)**

Divine favor is released according to the sovereign will of God. Just as there is a due date for a pregnant woman to give birth, there is an assigned time for divine favor to be released in your life.

For every promise, for every purpose, for every prophecy, and for every dream, there is a set time for manifestation. That is to say, there is an appointed time for that word or that promise or that dream to be manifested, and it is always the right time.

There is an appointed time for God to release divine favor to establish His particular purpose.

At that appointed time, there are some things that you can expect:

- You can expect some supernatural things to happen.

- You can expect the impossible to be made possible.

- You can expect God to move in ways that will boggle your mind.

- You can expect reformation and transformation.

Thou shalt arise and have mercy upon Zion: for the time to favor her, yea, the set time, is come. (**Psalm 102:13**)

Your expectation must never be based on who you use to be, but it should be based on who you shall become. The Bible declares that your position in Christ makes you eligible for the favor of God.

Because you are in Christ, you are Abraham's seed.

> *And if ye be Christ's, then are ye Abraham's seed, and heirs according to the promise.* **(Galatians 3:29 KJV)**

A life of favor is what God has destined for all believers in Christ.

The favor of God is the blessing of Abraham resting on your life. You are included in the covenant that God made with Abraham. God's favor will locate you wherever you are.

When God releases His favor upon your life, nothing and no one can stop you.

- Relatives can't stop you.
- Betrayal can't exclude you.
- Hard times can't disqualify you.
- Setbacks can't take it from you.
- Prison can't disbar you.

When it is your set time for God to release His favor upon you, there is nothing that can stop it from reaching you. Delays cannot take it away from you. As believers, we should always expect God to favor us. Expectation should be nurtured with preparation.

There is also an appointed place for manifestation.

- The lepers had to go outside the gate
- The disciples had to launch out into the deep
- Abraham had to go to a particular land

Often, we get discouraged because it does not happen according to our timeline. You need to walk in assurance during your waiting period. Every pregnancy has to endure a waiting period before the right time of delivery. Like the pregnant mother, you must wait on God for your set time of divine favor.

The Lord uses natural examples to show us how to prepare for the set time of favor. When a seed is sown, there is a process that the seed goes through before there can be a harvest. It is almost incomprehensible to think that a dormant seed can produce life when it is buried in the soil. Yet, within an hour of being sown, the process begins for the seed to germinate. Within ten hours, the seed begins to change, and sometimes in less than twenty-four hours, the seed begins to show visible signs of growth and development. It is a puzzling mystery, yet the seed produces life within a set time.

But as surely as the seed is planted, if it is kept in the ground and properly cared for, there will be a due season, and the harvest will come. The expected harvest requires preparation. You prepare for your harvest when you walk uprightly before God. Prepare your soil, and you shall reap the harvest of your preparation. Preparation is the key to success.

> *For the LORD God is a sun and shield: the LORD will give grace and glory: no good thing will he withhold from them that walk uprightly.* **(Psalm 84:11 KJV)**

Uprightness is measured in accordance to your obedience to the word of God. Expectation without preparation is an exercise in futility. Expecting to reap where you have not sown is the perfect setup for failure. Uprightness is a seed that brings forth a bountiful harvest.

Abraham walked with uprightness and was obedient to the instructions that he received from God. Obedience took him into strange and unfamiliar territory.

Expectation without preparation is an exercise in futility.

But in this hour, God is looking for some people who don't mind stepping out into the unknown. You must be willing to cut the umbilical cord and trust God to be your source of life. We must be willing to leave the comfort and familiarity of the womb. Many of us allow the comfort and familiarity of the womb to thwart our expectations. We do not want to cut the umbilical cord and are quite comfortable as long as we are attached to the womb. Oftentimes, obedience to the word of God requires a detachment from what seems safe and familiar. We must realize that even though life begins in the womb, it is lived outside the womb.

Poverty and lack are contradictions to the sentiments of God for mankind. The divine mandate declares that there is an open door to victory for anyone who is willing to enter through the door. Faith is the main door that leads to the opening of so many other doors. However, to effectively navigate your way through the corridors of faith, you must be willing to move from where you are to where you need to be.

The favor of God on your life enables you to win battles that are impossible for you to win using only your own strength. God's favor is a shield around you that provides protection from the onslaught of the enemy.

Psalm 5:12 says, "For thou, Lord, wilt bless the righteous; with favor wilt thou compass him as with a shield."

Your divine lineage puts you in the lineage of the righteous. You are the righteousness of God. You are the seed of Abraham.

> *And if ye be Christ's, then are ye Abraham's seed, and heirs according to the promise.* **(Galatians 3:29 KJV)**

When the favor of God is upon you, you can walk with your head held high even in the storms of life.

- Divine favor can turn adversity into victory.

- Divine favor introduces you to purpose.

- Divine favor singles you out for divine attention, and it brings you from the back of the line to the front.

- Divine favor does not care about your limitations or your history.

- Divine favor puts you in the right place at the right time and allows you to be noticed.

- Divine favor takes you from being a nobody to be a somebody.

- Divine favor establishes protection over your life.

- Divine favor brings provisions into your life.

- Divine favor causes you to recover your loss.

- Divine favor changes your story.

God's favor causes you to be promoted even when you are not qualified and gives you blessings even though you do not deserve them. It brings you out of prison even though you were given a life sentence.

When the favor of God goes before you, it opens doors that no man can shut, and it opens doors that men say are impossible to open. The favor of God will orchestrate amazing opportunities to get you through the door God wants you to go through.

Your set time of favor has come!

Get ready to be released into your *kairos season* of uncommon favor!

Get ready for elevation and promotion!

Get ready for increase!

It doth not yet appear but God has a plan for your life. He knows where He is taking you.

Get ready to *break forth*. This is your set time!

CHAPTER 5

HIDDEN GREATNESS

The Bible tells us about a woman who experienced "Misplaced Identity Syndrome (MIS)" that caused her to live a substandard life, but God used her saga to mold and shape her into the woman that He had destined her to be. It's a story about a woman who lived a life of insignificance until she was arrested by purpose and released into her destiny. Her life was dubbed with darkness, but at a *kairos* moment, a moment when time intersected with purpose, she emerged from utter darkness unto a stage where she had to shine for the glory of God.

The Bible says this woman was a harlot—a prostitute. She practiced ritual prostitution or what some call commercial prostitution. She was ignorant of her purpose and she had accepted a life that was driven by utter darkness. She became a prostitute, who was looking for love in the wrong places, and she sold her body for money to the highest bidder. She was totally detached from purpose.

"Misplaced Identity Syndrome" is a condition that fosters ignorance of your identity and promotes feelings of unworthiness. It is a demonic mindset that keeps you in bondage to prevent you from *breaking forth* into your purpose. MIS separates you from purpose and causes you to live a life that is outside the will of God. The enemy knows that if he can saturate your mind with a distorted image of self, you will never live the high impact life.

> *The thief cometh not, but for to steal, and to kill, and to destroy: I am come that they might have life, and that they might have it more abundantly.* **(John 10:10 KJV)**

The devil wants you to be impotent and ignorant of your true worth. If he can get you to believe that you are less than who God says you are, he can keep you in chains and shackles for the rest of your life.

Can you imagine the pain and the low self-esteem that this woman endured? She slept with different men every day and night. Maybe she was praying, "God deliver me, please." Maybe she was hoping that, one day, her circumstance would change. Maybe she wanted to take the red light down and replace it with the light of God. Maybe she wanted to die every time she felt a strange hand on her body. Maybe she felt like stepping out of her body every time she allowed the penetration of sin to pollute her being. Maybe she hated herself but she couldn't find a reason to stop. Maybe you find yourself in the same position as this woman—trapped and bound.

- Maybe it is the drugs.

- Maybe it is the cigarettes.

- Maybe it is the alcohol.

- Maybe it is the loneliness.
- Maybe it is the rejection.
- Maybe it is the molestation.
- Maybe it's the rape that you re-live everyday.
- Maybe it is the poverty.
- Maybe it's the depression.
- Maybe it's just life.

All of the above can cause you to lose touch with who you really are. As you are reading this book, I want you to stop for a minute and declare, "This is my time to *break forth* from Misplaced Identity Syndrome and unleash the 'Hidden Greatness' that is inside me!"

When you break forth into your kairos season, you convert your fears and your doubts into courage and faith.

By faith the walls of Jericho fell, after they were compassed about seven days. By faith the harlot Rahab perished not with them that believed not, when she had received the spies with peace. **(Hebrews 11:30–31 KJV)**

Let's talk about Rahab, the woman who had "hidden greatness" buried inside her. She lived a life of insignificance until she was introduced to her purpose. She was designed to accommodate God's purpose but spent a period of her life pleasing men instead of God.

There are certain occupations that we associate with

certain biblical characters. To say a name immediately brings a certain occupation to mind.

- Abraham was a herdsman.
- David was a shepherd.
- Nehemiah was a cupbearer.
- Isaiah was a prophet.
- Peter was a fisherman.
- Herod was a king.
- Esther was a queen.

Rahab was the harlot, the prostitute, the lady of the night, the one with whom many church folk would not want to associate.

The wonderful thing is, it is not what you used to be that matters; it is who you are going to be. No matter how many times you have missed the mark, you are still a purpose carrier. Your present circumstance does not define who you are. God Himself has ordained your purpose even before you were born.

***It is not what you used to be that matters;
it is who you are going to be.***

Before I formed thee in the belly I knew thee; and before thou camest forth out of the womb I sanctified thee, and I ordained thee a prophet unto the nations. **(Jeremiah 1:5 KJV)**

The enemy will always try to rob you of your purpose. He wants to kill the ministry inside you. Rahab was living her life, but spiritually, she was devoid of life. She was dead in her sins. Her circumstances brought her to a place where doom was hanging over her head—Jericho. Naturally and spiritually she was operating in areas that were tightly shut off from the will of God. There were walls that separated her from the will of God that needed to come down.

There is a Jericho wall that we all must encounter in life.

Rahab probably had given up any hope of ever turning her life around, but God had a plan for her life. There is a *kairos* moment when time intersects with divine purpose and you enter in a new season.

Praise the Lord!

> *Behold, at that time I will undo all that afflict thee: and I will save her that halteth and gather her that was driven out; and I will get them praise and fame in every land where they have been put to shame.* **(Zephaniah 3:19 KJV)**

God can turn shame to glory in one shining moment of redemption.

So many rise every day wondering why death did not rescue them in the night from the depression and anxiety that greeted them in the morning. They crave for the stranger who will lend a body to be the opiate that will satisfy the emptiness and endless longing for acceptance and recognition. They become slaves to activities of fleshly gain hoping to get rid of the pain from "Misplaced Identity Syndrome" and undiscovered purpose.

There is a great multitude walking around with untapped reservoirs of greatness. Interestingly, it is only after God allows us to experience some major eruptions in life that we *break forth* into an awareness of purpose and self-discovery. When we experience these volcanic eruptions, there is a shaking that causes detachment and "things" that were seemingly attached to our souls are loosened and fall from us. From the ashes we emerge, with such beauty that transcends cosmetic overlays.

> *To appoint unto them that mourn in Zion, to give unto them beauty for ashes, the oil of joy for mourning, the garment of praise for the spirit of heaviness; that they might be called trees of righteousness, the planting of the LORD, that he might be glorified.* **(Isaiah 61:3 KJV)**

There might be days when you wake up and it feels as if your mind is locked in a tunnel, everything seems to be upside down, and you can feel the bumps and jolts that come with intense turbulence. During these times, you must fasten your belt, adjust your altitude, and get ready to *break forth* above the cumulus clouds of despair into a zone of stability and security that is consistent with God's plan for your life.

If you are experiencing spiritual atmospheric instability, with unpredictable moments of unrest and disorder, you need to know without any reservation or doubt that you are made to win. You are an overcomer. You are more than a conqueror. You are the indomitable image of your Creator. You are unassailable and empowered to surmount every obstacle. You can subdue every force from hell that threatens your destiny. You can weather any storm. Remember, you have "hidden greatness" inside you, and this is your season to *break forth*.

> **You can subdue every force from hell that threatens your destiny.**

There is an omnipotent, loving God with whom absolutely nothing is impossible. He is El Gibbor, the Mighty God. He is Jehovah Mephalti, your Deliverer. There is nothing that He cannot do. He is your battle-axe who wins every battle on behalf of His people.

> *Thou art my battle axe and weapons of war.* **(Jeremiah 51:20 KJV)**

He is bigger than all your problems, bigger than all your fears, bigger than any mountain in your life. He is bigger than your past and greater than your future.

God doesn't go around referring to Moses as "Moses the Murderer" when He speaks of great faith. God doesn't go around referring to Abraham as "Abraham the Liar" when he speaks of great faith. In His hall of faith, He refers to no one by their past profession. However, when it comes to Rahab, God says, "Rahab the Harlot."

No matter how wretched your past may be, you are designed to accommodate God's purpose for your life. You are still a carrier of "hidden greatness" and God has great plans for you. Only those who have gone through extreme turbulence in their lives are inducted in God's Hall of Faith. Rahab's turbulent past prepared her for her great future.

> **Your past does not have to control your future.**

She has been memorialized in chapter 11 of the book of Hebrews, next to Moses and Abraham and Sarah. Yes, Rahab was a harlot, but when she was connected to her purpose, she was able to *break forth* into greatness. Ignorance of her real purpose plagued her for a while, but when she was inducted into God's army, she embraced the call to destiny. She probably thought her greatness was tied to how many men she could sleep with and collect. Like many who are looking for love and validation in the wrong place, she entertained strange men for a few moments of pleasure. God had already destined her for greatness and, at the appointed time, she was released into a *kairos season* of transformation and liberty.

> *Before I formed thee in the belly, I knew thee; and before thou camest forth out of the womb I sanctified thee, and I ordained thee a prophet unto the nations.* **(Jeremiah 1:5 KJV)**

It wasn't until purpose was revealed to Rahab that she discovered that her destiny was not to be a harlot but a kingdom appointee. God used Rahab the Harlot, to save Israel. God summoned her to the battlefield and she found herself amid warfare that caused what was inside her to *break forth*.

Do not despise the warfare that you are going through, for it can bring forth the best in you.

Just like Rahab, you are a kingdom appointee. You were born for greatness. When purpose knocked on her door, she opened the door to her destiny. God converted the red light at the window to the scarlet cord.

Your destiny was sanctioned in the bosom of eternity. The good news is God doesn't see you as you are. He sees you as you shall become. He sees you according to your prophetic destiny. You were born to make a difference. Your story can change. You don't have to settle anymore. You can rise above your circumstance. You do not have to accept life on the enemy's terms anymore. Yes, you might have been a prostitute, you might have been addicted to drugs, you might have lived a life that was not pleasing to God, you might have been "a whatsoever or a whosoever," but God has a great plan for your life.

I declare to you that you are better than your circumstance. You are not your issue.

Your issue is a temporary setback for a major comeback.

You are made in the image and likeness of God, and you are coded with greatness inside you.

In Rahab, I see the power of God that can transform the lives of those who come to know Him. Just as the Lord changed this woman, He can rehabilitate any life that is brought to Him. Regardless of how wicked, how broken, how lost, or how wretched you may be, God can change you. You can *break forth* into greatness.

Chapter 6

IN THE ROUGH

Most of us have probably heard the term "diamond in the rough." This phrase is used to refer to a person who has extraordinary hidden characteristics and potential but has not yet gone through the process of development that would make him or her noticeable in a crowd.

It is a metaphorical phrase used to demonstrate that the person may seem ordinary at first glance, but their true beauty as a diamond is only realized through the cutting-and-polishing process. In other words, they have so much hidden on the inside of them, but they need to submit to a finishing process that would expose their brilliance and make them shine.

You, like Rahab, might be disconnected from your purpose. You might be going through some things in your life right now. There might be some powerful eruptions going on, but you need to know this: you are a diamond in the rough! You are about to shine like never before. Your eruptions were for good and not for bad.

Whatever you are experiencing now is divinely sanctioned to prepare you for the next season of your life.

God is preparing you for your "greater." *Kairos seasons* come without warnings and are always tied to God's divine plan for your life. Such seasons are supernaturally directed and require a demonstration of faith, with reckless abandon and action, that is indicative of total surrender. You are a diamond in the rough, and every diamond must experience turbulence and pressure in order to *break forth*.

Whatever you are experiencing now is divinely sanctioned to prepare you for the next season of your life.

Diamonds don't automatically shine and sparkle. Diamonds that are uncut are rough and aren't like the diamonds we wear as adornment. Only the cut diamonds sparkle. A diamond has to be cut by someone who is skilled in diamond cutting for it to sparkle and reflect light. We must be cut by our "Master Designer" in order to sparkle and reflect the light of Christ in the way that we should. Rahab was an uncut diamond in the rough until she was cut by the Sovereign Lord, the great "Master Designer," God Almighty.

One of the characteristics of a diamond is its clarity. That involves whether any impurities or inclusions are present in the diamond. Depending on its visibility, the grade of a diamond will go up or down. Any impurities found in you will present a credibility issue and could greatly affect your witness. Some impurities may not be visible to the naked eye, but they are clearly seen by God.

> *For the LORD seeth not as man seeth; for man looketh on the outward appearance, but the LORD looketh on the heart.*
> **(1 Samuel 16:7 KJV)**

Diamonds are carried to the surface of the earth by volcanic eruptions; very few diamonds survive the hazardous journey from the depths of the earth to reach the surface.

The word diamond in the Greek language translates as *adamas*, which means unconquerable and indestructible. There is a process that must be endured for a diamond to emerge.

There is a process that must be endured for a diamond to emerge.

A diamond starts out as a common chunk of coal and can only become a diamond if a tremendous amount of pressure is applied.

The real beauty breaks forth after the diamond endures the process of heating, pressuring, and cutting.

If you are reading this book, you need to know that God will allow you to experience pressure so you can endure the process of transformation from the unprocessed you to a brilliant diamond. In addition to extreme pressure, there must be some cutting. There has to be a circumcision of the flesh from the spirit. The Holy Spirit cuts away those things in our lives that do not glorify God and makes us more valuable to reflect the light and character of Christ.

> *And we know that all things work together for good to them that love God, to them who are the called according to his purpose.*
> **(Romans 8:28 KJV)**

The great purpose of God's plan is that every one of his chosen people, the most obscure and anonymous, the people who stumbled—like Rahab, David, the woman at the well, you, and, me—will survive the eruptions and the pressures of life to brilliantly shine and be great witnesses for God.

There are great struggles that we might have to experience on the journey to *breaking forth.* We must overcome the forces within ourselves and those without that would cause us to abort the plan of God for our lives. We cannot allow the weight and the discouragement of trials to cause us to surrender to defeat.

> *Wherefore seeing we also are compassed about with so great a cloud of witnesses, let us lay aside every weight, and the sin which doth so easily beset us, and let us run with patience the race that is set before us.* **(Hebrews 12:1 KJV)**

We must learn lessons from disappointments and setbacks and recognize the value of every delay that comes our way. The process of becoming a diamond is long and enduring, but in time, what was nothing more than a dead piece of coal *breaks forth* to sparkle and shine.

We must learn lessons from disappointments and setbacks and recognize the value of every delay that comes our way.

Inasmuch as God has set aside a prescribed plan for your life, you will have to make the choice to endure the journey to the top. You have to make the choice to trade in your pain, your hurt, your sorrow, and your shame for a life of liberation and joy. Once you have made the trade, you will begin to experience a newness that will distance you from your past and introduce you to your real self.

Rahab had to go through a finishing process to be transformed into the person that God ordained her to be. We must be willing to endure the force of pressure, the degree of heat, the pain of cutting, and the friction of polishing so we can be fully transformed into vessels of honor. The pain of suffering through the process is the prelude to the gain of triumph.

The journey to newness requires that you surrender to the potter's wheel. The old you might have been engulfed and corrupted by deceitful desires that alienated you from your purpose and locked you in a prison of reduction and devaluation. The wonderful news is God does not only save us from hell. He saves us from ourselves.

> *Behold, the LORD'S hand is not shortened, that it cannot save; neither his ear heavy, that it cannot hear.* **(Isaiah 59:1 KJV)**

The course of our lives is the means to the end of God's predestined plan for each person—seasons of ups and downs, sickness and health, plenty and little, success and failure, but in every season, God's plan remains intact.

You might be going through some things right now but God has a plan! You might be in the rough right now, but God has a plan. God's purpose comes with a prescribed plan. God has a plan for your life.

> *For I know the thoughts that I think toward you, saith the LORD, thoughts of peace, and not of evil, to give you an expected end.* **(Jeremiah 29:11 KJV)**

God will allow you to go through some things to mold and shape you. But through it all, you must embrace the truth that God knows more about you than you know about yourself. He is the "Expert Manufacturer" who has designed you according to the plan He has for your life. Your days on earth are according to His divine schedule, and He has sovereignty over your life. God released you out of the bosom of eternity into your mother's womb to carry out a specific assignment here on earth.

> *Before I formed thee in the belly I knew thee; and before thou camest forth out of the womb I sanctified thee, and I ordained thee a prophet unto the nations.* **(Jeremiah 1:5 KJV)**

God released you out of the bosom of eternity into your mother's womb to carry out a specific assignment here on earth.

The Bible tells us in Psalm 139 that we are fearfully and wonderfully formed. That means that you were well carefully considered, deliberately planned, meticulously fashioned, and intricately designed by and for God. There is some special stuff that God put inside you. You were sent here with a specific genetic coding, and that genetic coding is found in your blood. The consistency and the composition of your blood are coded to accommodate God's purpose for your life. The very best of God is in you. Spiritually, you have God's DNA, which comes with a genetic coding and instructions for your development.

> *And the LORD God formed man of the dust of the ground and breathed into his nostrils the breath of life; and man became a living soul.* **(Genesis 2:7 KJV)**

I will submit to you that when God blew into man *the breath of life*, what was in God went into man, and it is the same breath that is in you. God only breathed one time into man, and that same breath has prevailed and sustained humanity since the beginning of time. The *breath of life* was more than just air as we know it. It is the substance by which we are able to *break forth* into purpose. It was more than just oxygen.

The *breath of life* had a certain consistency that when God released it, it had inherent creative power to put things in place and in order. It bears a certain coding that can organize the organism. It numbers the very hairs on your head. It strategically put lungs, liver, heart, and kidneys in place and set the body in order. God's breath releases a spiritual genetic coding that transcribes purpose and intent of our lives.

God knows why He released you into the earthly realm. He knows what your assignment is here on earth. He has designed you to carry out that specific assignment. Even when your life is embedded with problems and you are deep in the *rough*, you are still a purpose carrier. You are designed to withstand the journey of the *rough*. The *rough* is a place of perfecting and shaping.

Even when your life is embedded with problems and you are deep in the rough, you are still a purpose carrier.

If you endure the process, you will *break forth* into your destiny.

Chapter 7

VICTORY SHINE

You might have been in a slump and you feel like you are all out of options. It might seem as if God has not heard your prayers and He really doesn't care enough to come to your rescue. At the very moment when you are seemingly overwhelmed with your present circumstance, this is the very time you will get a breakthrough so you can *break forth*. God has given you the measure of grace that can sustain you through your valley season and enable you to bounce back from your funk.

> *And he said unto me, my grace is sufficient for thee: for my strength is made perfect in weakness.* **(2 Corinthians 12:9 KJV)**

This is your season to *break forth*. Your time for change has come. A chicken is hatched, but it must spend a certain amount of time in the shell. It is a time of development and growth. Eventually the chicken must break out of the shell to operate and function according to the purpose for which it was born. If it stayed in the shell forever, it would abort its purpose. Just as the chicken must *break forth* out of its shell, you too must *break forth* into your destiny.

It is time for you go higher. You must *break forth* out of whatever shell that has been restricting you and move into a higher dimension of purpose.

> **You must break forth out of whatever shell that has been restricting you and move into a higher dimension of purpose.**

To focus on what lies ahead of you, or what lies in front of you, without addressing and releasing what is inside of you is a travesty that leads to the breakdown of humanity. There is a *kairos season* that facilitates the breaking forth of gifts, talents, and ideas for those who dare to puncture the bubble in which they have been trapped.

You have been hiding in that shell too long. It's time for you to *break forth*. If you stay where you are, you will never get to the next rung of the ladder.

> *Arise, shine; for thy light is come, and the glory of the LORD is risen upon thee.*
> **(Isaiah 60:1 KJV)**

Deep down inside you is the capacity to *break forth* and shine through your darkest moment. You might be struggling with issues. You might be going through some things and not understand your present circumstance. You might be experiencing some eruptions in your life. You try to do the right thing, but major eruptions keep coming. There might be some interferences and intrusions in your life that have created a whirlwind of chaos, and it seems as if there is no help in sight.

The truth is every eruption in your life is designed to

enlarge your capacity to *break forth* and reveal the hidden greatness that is in you.

Every eruption in your life is designed to enlarge your capacity to break forth and reveal the hidden greatness that is in you.

There are times in life when God will allow you to experience turbulence before it gets to be smooth sailing. Amid those dark and trying times, God is perfecting you for your destiny. It is in the turmoil and through the deep anguish of life that the true you is given the opportunity to *break forth* with awesome resilience and strength of character.

> My brethren, count it all joy when ye fall into divers temptations; Knowing this, that the trying of your faith worketh patience. But let patience have her perfect work, that ye may be perfect and entire, wanting nothing. **(James 1:2–4 KJV)**

Some of you have experienced major turbulence and have suffered instability, disruption, and turmoil. Take joy in knowing that your turbulent journey has provided extensive preparation for your destination. Despite major eruptions and turbulence, your destiny is great. You shall *break forth* into purpose. You are about to come from the bottom to the top.

Your turbulent journey has provided extensive preparation for your destination.

You can overcome every eruption that is going on in your life. You are about to *break forth*! You belong to God, and He has already fixed it so you can win. Even if the eruptions cause you to explode into a million pieces, God is the potter, and He can put you back together again. Even if you fall like Humpty Dumpty, God is the omnipotent, all-able God, and He can reassemble every broken piece.

> *But now thus saith the LORD that created thee, O Jacob, and he that formed thee, O Israel, Fear not: for I have redeemed thee, I have called thee by thy name; thou art mine. When thou passest through the waters, I will be with thee; and through the rivers, they shall not overflow thee: when thou walkest through the fire, thou shalt not be burned; neither shall the flame kindle upon thee.*
> **(Isaiah 43:1–3 KJV)**

Breaking Forth is a change that produces an increase in levels and a stretch into new dimensions of growth and development. It is accepting your divine impregnation and giving birth to the embryonic seed of greatness that has kicked the walls of the womb of your mind, looking to escape. *Breaking Forth* sends signals to the universe that the season of darkness has come to an end and the light of a new day prevails.

God made you to be a bright light to emit rays of hope that will bring glory and honor to His name even in the darkest moments of your life. He made you to be distinctive and to be conspicuous for your uniqueness. In life, there are seasons when there is a dimming of the inner flame of strength, but you are never out of reach of victory.

You are made to dispel darkness and to brighten your sphere of influence by reflecting the character of God.

> *Ye are the light of the world. A city that is set on a hill cannot be hid. Neither do men light a candle, and put it under a bushel, but on a candlestick; and it giveth light unto all that are in the house. ⁱ⁶ Let your light so shine before men, that they may see your good works, and glorify your Father which is in heaven.* **(Matthew 5:14–16 KJV)**

Do not allow your circumstance to prevent you from shining. You need to submerge your mind in the revelation that every eruption in your life was designed to increase your brilliance as you shine.

You need to tell the adversary that you are about to surface and when you do his kingdom is in trouble.

I believe that most of us do not understand the power and the capacity we have as overcomers. You were born to endure pressure. You have grit. Mediocrity is not your station. Complacency is not your portion. You were not born to accept a second-class existence. You were born to shine!

Sometimes, we allow our circumstances to cause us to experience identity crisis, and we forget who we are and end up settling for less than what God has for us.

God is about to take you out of obscurity. The end of your story shall be different from the beginning. You are about to exceed limits that you thought you did not have the capacity to exceed.

The devil will try to launch his warfare tactics against you, but try as he might, he cannot prevail against you—unless you give him permission to do so. He does not want you to shine. He wants you to live a life that is dim and without victory. He will lay snares with the intent to sabotage your destiny. But as you shine, your light will be so bright that you can see the snares of oppression and depression, snares of temptation and addiction, and snares of failure and defeat. His job description is to steal, kill, and destroy. Your job description is to have dominion over the works of the enemy.

> *Behold, I give unto you power to tread on serpents and scorpions, and over all the power of the enemy: and nothing shall by any means hurt you.* **(Luke 10:19 KJV)**

May I remind you that you are an overcomer. You can overcome every snare that the enemy sets for you.

- You can overcome oppression and depression.
- You can overcome every addiction.
- You can overcome low self-esteem.
- You can overcome fornication.
- You can overcome sexual promiscuity.
- You can overcome pain and suffering.

Newsflash: God fixed it so you can win in the battle.

This is the season for you to take authority over every shackle that has had you bound. It is time for you to evict every trespassing agent that has entered your mind with the propaganda of failure and defeat. Your days of being held captive to defeat must come to an end. Your destiny is waiting for you to start the journey of triumph and to say goodbye to obscurity and anonymity.

It's time to awake the sleeping giant inside you. You must turn on that dormant ability that has been buried under issues and stuff. It's time to expose your exceptional brilliance so the intense brightness of your soul can radiate in your sphere of influence.

God is about progression and not regression. Elevation and expansion will be yours when you aptly unlock your potential. It is about your transformation and perfection as you go from glory to glory. It is about being a better you. It is about digging deep on the inside and commanding your soul to advance in a realm you have never been before.

You cannot get stuck on yesterday's anointing. Yesterday's anointing will never unlock anything for you today. When you are obsessed with the past, you can never see the future. Some of us are so comfortable with our past that we refuse to move beyond where we have been for years. You don't have to function with leftover anointing. God wants to give you fresh oil for you to soar above yesterday's accomplishment.

You cannot get stuck on yesterday's anointing. Yesterday's anointing will never unlock anything for you today.

Brethren, I count not myself to have apprehended: but this one thing I do, forgetting those things which are behind, and reaching forth unto those things which are before, I press toward the mark for the prize of the high calling of God in Christ Jesus. **(Philippians 3:13–14 KJV)**

Many people do not know who they are from God's perspective. As a result, they are ignorant of their capabilities. They only know who they are from man's perspective. That is why so many are operating far below the level of their abilities and are detached from purpose. They have relied on another human being to define who they are and have submitted to the beliefs and opinions of others.

The word of God defines who you are, and it provides you with a clear picture of the masterpiece that God designed when He made you. God did not make an empty shell without gifts and talents and no capacity to accomplish great feats in life. The Bible presents a plethora of awesome truths about how you can transform your mind from a cesspool of apathy and lethargy to become all that God wants you to be.

Be encouraged and walk in confidence. The real you is about to *break forth,* and you shall shine for the glory of God.

Chapter 8

THE REWARDS OF DILIGENCE

As children of the Most High God, we are to lead productive lives and *break forth* with good success. We are to lead in our area of gifting, live victorious lives, and bring honor and glory to God. As kingdom citizens, we are to lead by example. Every citizen of any kingdom should reflect the mindset of the King.

God, in His sovereignty, released a biblical constitution for His kingdom citizens. He expects His people to advance His kingdom and to take dominion over every realm held captive by the enemy. In order to *break forth* into your *kairos season* of divine release, there must be a diligent effort to extricate self from the grip of a darkness that is weaved in complacency and lethargy. We have to be diligent in our affairs. Verbal confessions of success must be the segue to intentional actions directed to achieve excellence. God rewards diligent stewardship, and more is given unto those who prove to excel in this area.

The Rewards of Diligence

> *He that is faithful in that which is least is faithful also in much: and he that is unjust in the least is unjust also in much. If therefore ye have not been faithful in the unrighteous mammon, who will commit to your trust the true riches?* **(Luke 16:10–11 KJV)**

This is the age of shortcuts and microwaves. Many are living in the throes of a society where the expectation is to reap a harvest without sowing. The bedrock principle of breaking forth into the *kairos season* is eliminating shortcuts that deny you the opportunity to endure the process of growth and development.

In the biblical constitution for kingdom citizens, the ant teaches us the danger of laziness in our lives. God uses the most unlikely teaching source to emphasize the importance of being diligent. For you to obtain the rewards of diligence, you must develop the discipline of the ant.

Self-motivation is indeed one of the most valuable lessons that we can learn from this creature which personifies the epitome of diligence. *Breaking forth* into your *kairos season* requires diligence that is purposeful and intentional. The ant has no supervisor—there is no boss to supervise this self-directed leader. There are no clocks to punch that govern its day's work. It remains focused and maximizes the time.

> *Go to the ant, thou sluggard; consider her ways, and be wise: Which having no guide, overseer, or ruler, Provideth her meat in the summer, and gathereth her food in the harvest. How long wilt thou sleep, O sluggard? when wilt thou arise out of thy sleep?* **(Proverbs 6:6–9 KJV)**

Breaking Forth

There is a level of responsibility that is required of you as a kingdom citizen. Just as the ant works for the good of the ant kingdom, you are expected to operate with a level of diligence and maturity that will bring increase into your life. Any agenda that does not promote diligence compromises access into your *kairos season* of advancement.

One of the many lessons that we learn from the ant is the value of preparation. If you are to *break forth* into your season of growth and development, you must prepare for opportunities that are conducive to elevation. The ant teaches a valuable lesson in maximization of time: *"Provides her supplies in the summer and gathers her food in the harvest"* **(Proverbs 6:8).**

The wisest man, King Solomon, asks the question in the book of Proverbs: "How long will you slumber, O sluggard? When will you rise from your sleep?" (Proverbs 6:9). He goes on to give us the outcome of one who does not have the diligence of the ant: *"So shall your poverty come on you like a prowler, and your need like an armed man"* **(Proverbs 6:11).**

Whenever we exchange diligence for laziness, we open the door to poverty.

Those who pattern their lives after the ant always experience good success. Fruitfulness is the reward of diligence. There is a *kairos* moment when time intersects with God's divine purpose. It requires diligence and intentional action to maximize the moment. Laziness in any form, whether it be spiritual or physical, is a threat to your destiny. Go to the ant! "Consider her ways and be wise"!

Laziness in any form, whether it be spiritual or physical is a threat to your destiny.

We are a microwave society. Getting by is the standard now for many believers. Our impatience will not allow for the process of *breaking forth* to be manifested in our lives. The greatness that God has placed on the inside us suffers from self-directed sabotage that operates from a platform of impatience.

Success does not come by osmosis and is the offspring of diligence.

You must use the keys that will open the doors to good success. Standing outside the door looking in will not allow you to access what's behind the door.

- This is no time for star gazing.

- It's no time for being a spectator.

- It's no time for great ideas without working the plan.

You will never *break forth* into your God-given purpose by accident. You have to diligently seek after purpose. Your success cannot be bought in a store at the lotto station. You will not be so privileged to bump into success on the way to kicking back and chilling. It is not going to fall out of the sky into your lap. You cannot track it through UPS or FedEx for next-day air delivery. It is earned by those who seek after it with diligence and steadfastness of heart.

The Bible gives us the profile of Joshua, who had the discipline of the ant, coupled with a commitment to righteousness. He was a spiritual giant who led the children of Israel into the promised land. He was rewarded for his diligence.

> *This book of the law shall not depart out of thy mouth; but thou shalt meditate therein day and night, that thou mayest observe to do according to all that is written therein: for then thou shalt make thy way prosperous, and then thou shalt have good success.* **(Joshua 1:8 KJV)**

The mechanic that would perfect his work must first sharpen his tools. As believers, we must sharpen our tools. To maximize your *kairos season* and to be successful in what God has called you to do, you must be diligent. Great works are accomplished not just by strength but by diligence.

We will look at the profile of Joshua, a man whose resume was highlighted by good success.

- He diligently followed Moses, his leader, until he died.

- He diligently served Moses with devotion for God.

- He diligently executed his duties with precision.

- He diligently focused on the vision from God.

- He diligently finished whatever he put his hands to do.

- He diligently handled warfare as a strong military leader.

- He diligently faced the giants and was not afraid of them.
- He diligently took authority over the walls of Jericho.

Moses's death was the beginning of a *kairos season* for Joshua, and God was about to take him into a higher dimension of ministry. He was used to doing things under the authority of Moses, but now he was being promoted to be the next authority. This would be a season in which Joshua would be stretched to go beyond where he had ever been. In this season, trust in God cannot waver. For Joshua to maximize his *kairos season* and be successful at what God had called him to do, he had to be diligent.

Any attempt to be successful without diligence is potential failure.

If you labor diligently, you can expect great rewards. Diligence must be your personal signature in everything you do. You must be known because of your diligence. You must be diligent in your personal lives, you must be diligent in your spiritual life, and you must be diligent in whatever office you hold in the kingdom of God.

The hand of the diligent will rule, but the lazy man will be put to forced labor.
(Proverbs 12:24 KJV)

Your effectiveness is measured by the impact you have on people's lives. It requires diligent investing of your time, your effort, your substance, and your energy in a way that will accomplish prescribed goals. You must develop the mindset of a winner. Again, you can look at the ant to learn how to yield results from your efforts.

In order to *break forth* into your *kairos season*, you will have to do some things that will require a lot of courage. Joshua had to face many enemies and handle severe adversity. You cannot be courageous if you are weak in your thoughts. To reap the rewards of diligence, you must have a strong mind. That means you have to be able to think correctly. You must be able to overcome your present reality and step out by faith and in faith.

It is impossible to maximize your *kairos season* if you do not think correctly. The way you think determines your success in life. To seek the rewards of diligence, your mind must be renewed so you can be transformed into a person who exemplifies diligence of character.

> *For as he thinketh in his heart, so is he.*
> **(Proverbs 23:7 KJV)**

Whatever you consistently think about is what you will inevitably become. If you think you're a success, you are. If you think you're a failure, you are. You are what you think you are. Your thoughts are the building blocks of who you are and what you will eventually become.

You are what you think you are!

You see, everything in life begins with a thought. Everything you see around began as a thought in the mind of a creator.

When God decided to create a universe, the thought of the universe began in His mind, and then, by the sheer power of His own omnipotence, He spoke the universe into existence. By the power of His own words and that which only began as a thought, He created everything.

Success begins in your mind, just as failure begins

there as well. But failure and success cannot live in the same place. You must choose which one you will enter into a lease agreement with. You can have laziness as a tenant, or you can have diligence. Which one are you going to give an occupancy permit?

Your mind is the place where successful living begins, and it is also the place where poverty dwells. The mind is the place where the devil will fight you the most, because he knows that once you make up your mind to trust God and move into your *kairos season* of development and expansion, he cannot deter you. He will send subliminal messages to the mind to trigger "Misplaced Identity Syndrome." If you see yourself as a grasshopper, you will never get to great heights. If you are afraid of giants, you will never be a giant killer. Your actions are indicative of how you identify yourself.

> **Your mind is the place where successful living begins, and it is also the place where poverty dwells.**

Joshua was not intimidated by giants. His diligence reflected the power that was working in him.

> **Your diligence reflects the power that is working in you.**

When you are pursuing the rewards of diligence, you cannot be afraid of adversity. You have to be willing to face adversity head-on and command it to bow to your purpose.

The word of God is the schoolteacher of diligence.

> *For the word of God is quick, and powerful, and sharper than any two-edged sword, piercing even to the dividing asunder of soul and spirit, and of the joints and marrow, and is a discerner of the thoughts and intents of the heart.* **(Hebrews 4:12 KJV)**

Obedience to the Word of God is the key to unlocking the abundance, the blessing, and the favor of God in your life. Your obedience to His word is reflected in your diligence. Doing the word of God is the prerequisite to receiving the reward from God.

Diligence is the mother of good success.

> *Seest thou a man diligent in his business? he shall stand before kings; he shall not stand before mean men.* **(Proverbs 22:29 KJV)**

> *How long wilt thou sleep, O sluggard? when wilt thou arise out of thy sleep? Yet a little sleep, a little slumber, a little folding of the hands to sleep: So shall thy poverty come as one that travelleth, and thy want as an armed man.* **(Proverbs 6:9–11 KJV)**

> *The soul of the sluggard desireth, and hath nothing: but the soul of the diligent shall be made fat.* **(Proverbs 13:4 KJV)**

Diligence is the path that you must take to secure the harvest of your kairos season.

The Rewards of Diligence

The rewards of diligence come to those who

- Change the way they think
- Change the way they speak
- Change the way they act

Jesus set the standard for us to be diligent in our affairs. His ministry was good success.

He was diligent in his business. He was not distracted by the naysayers. He was not distracted by temptation. He was not distracted by the attacks on His physical body. He was focused on purpose. When you are focused on purpose, you remain diligent in your affairs.

- You press harder.
- You work harder.
- You pray better.
- You love stronger.
- You dream bigger.
- You sacrifice greater.

When you are focused on purpose, you remain diligent in your affairs.

Breaking forth should never be an afterthought in your mind. You were destined to *break forth!*

Epilogue

When all is said and done, it is what you did with your time on earth that determines your destiny. Your destiny will testify to the choices you made and the path that you choose to walk. You were awakened so many mornings, you have lived so many hours, you have made millions of decisions, and you have made so many choices. How well did you use your time?

You are almost at the end of this book, and as you think about all that you have read, there are some questions you need to ask.

- Think back to the beginning of your journey. Have you given it all that you should have given? Did you stay the course?

- Think back to the days you felt like you couldn't go any further. Did you push yourself to go the extra mile?

- Think back to when people ignored and rejected you. Did you allow them to crush your dreams and minimize your vision?

- Think back to the first time you realized that there was greatness inside you. Did you execute a plan to expose that hidden greatness and to unlock the measure of your potential?

- Think back to things you did that disconnected you from your purpose. What did you stop and what did you start that would effectively help you to walk in your purpose?

- Think back to when you discovered that your social environment worked against your dream and minimized your vision. Did you step away from the crowd that limited your growth and development?

- Think back to when you were gripped with fear and was stuck in a place of inertia. Did you do everything to extricate yourself from the bonds of fear? Did you find a way to cultivate the courage that was needed to walk away?

- Think back to the time when apathy and indifference caused non-productivity to be on your personal resume. Did you create an action plan that required you to move from where you were to where you needed to be?

As you reflect on your journey, there are so many questions that might be posed. Did you do this or did you do that? How did you handle this, or how did you handle that? The past presents a true picture of our choices, but it does not command that we live there. You have the power to rewrite your story and live a life that laughs at the dark past and celebrates a bright future.

Lessons learned from the past should equip us with wisdom to extricate ourselves from the destiny blockers that seek to rob us of our rightful place in history. We must make the choice to live in an environment that is conducive to our growth and development. We must be mindful that God holds us responsible and He expects proper stewardship of the gifts and talents that He sovereignly bestowed upon us.

It's important to note that despite the potential of the seed, the maximization of that seed is greatly affected by its environment. We are challenged to examine our lives and to make the necessary adjustments that will provide a suitable environment for maximizing the *kairos season.* We must diligently pursue the calling of God and occupy the office that is specifically designed to accommodate the purpose of God.

> *I must work the works of him that sent me, while it is day: the night cometh, when no man can work.* **(John 9:4 KJV)**

Visions and dreams without nurturing and steadfast work diminishes our level of accomplishment. It is the work that we do that determines our success. The work that we do shall one day be judged by the "One" who dispatched us to the workstations of life. We will have to answer to our Creator one day on how we did. We shall be graded on our stewardship and we will have to answer hard questions. If we did well, we will hear, "Well done." If not, we would have failed the test and be subject to severe punishment.

> *His lord said unto him, Well done, good and faithful servant; thou hast been faithful over a few things, I will make thee ruler over many things: enter thou into the joy of thy lord. Then he which had received the one talent came and said, Lord, I knew thee that*

thou art an hard man, reaping where thou hast not sown, and gathering where thou hast not strawed: And I was afraid and went and hid thy talent in the earth: lo, there thou hast that is thine. His lord answered and said unto him, Thou wicked and slothful servant, thou knewest that I reap where I sowed not, and gather where I have not strawed: Thou oughtest therefore to have put my money to the exchangers, and then at my coming I should have received mine own with usury. Take therefore the talent from him and give it unto him which hath ten talents. For unto everyone that hath shall be given, and he shall have abundance: but from him that hath not shall be taken away even that which he hath. And cast ye the unprofitable servant into outer darkness: there shall be weeping and gnashing of teeth.
(Matthew 25:23–30 KJV)

Kudos to you for whatever you have accomplished in the past. While it is good to look back and to see a check mark in the completed column of your action plan, do not settle for history. It is not what you have done; it is what you are yet to do. Your desire to be a world-changer who will leave a deposit on earth should be the driving force to go beyond where you have been.

Every second, every moment, every hour, any time that is given to you should be used to break every shackle of self-imposed imprisonment. Do not allow the bars of failure and defeat to incarcerate and confine you to a life of mediocrity. You cannot undo what you have already done, but you can spend the rest of your life maximizing every moment of your allotted time. Your *kairos season* is now. Now is your time to excel above the ranks of the ordinary and the accustomed levels of the status quo.

> *Sing, O barren, thou that didst not bear;* **break forth** *into singing, and cry aloud, thou that didst not travail with child: for more are the children of the desolate than the children of the married wife, saith the LORD. Enlarge the place of thy tent, and let them stretch forth the curtains of thine habitations: spare not, lengthen thy cords, and strengthen thy stakes; For thou shalt* **break forth** *on the right hand and on the left...* **(Isaiah 54:1–3 KJV)**

Now is your time to *break forth* and maximize your *kairos season*!

Unshackle

Walk

Unleash

Enlarge

Maximize

Stretch

Leave a legacy on earth!

Break forth!

About the Author

Angela Marie Rucker, PhD, ThD, DD

Dr. Angela Rucker is an international minister, lecturer, and visionary leader.

Travelling extensively throughout the world, Dr. Rucker ministers restoration to people who are broken and void of purpose. Dr. Rucker deals with the real issues of life and presents an alternative to all of life struggles. The focus of her ministry is to teach people how to "walk in dominion" so they can discover self and move from brokenness to wholeness.

Dr. Rucker serves as the Assistant Pastor of Bride of Christ Church Ministries International, located in Mitchellville, MD. She is the president and chief executive officer of Cradle of H.O.P.E., Inc. Foundation.

Dr. Rucker earned a Doctorate in Theology from Andersonville Theological Seminary. She also earned a Doctor of Philosophy from Empowerment Theological Institute and Bible Seminary. She was awarded an Honorary Doctorate in Divinity from Eastern North Carolina Theological Institute.

Dr. Rucker and her husband, Benjamin, serve together as a team. They are called to go beyond geographical boundaries to teach and preach the uncompromising word of God. They travel together and plant many churches globally.

Printed in the United States
By Bookmasters